*I Am Just a Little Child,
Of This You Can Be Sure...*

Does It Still Hurt?

I Am "Just" A Little Child, Of This You Can Be Sure…

Does It Still Hurt?

Marie Parks Pinto, MSW, LSW, CRS
Illustrations by Miriam Mazzei

Full Court Press
Englewood Cliffs, New Jersey

First Edition

Copyright © 2012 by Marie Parks Pinto
Illustrations Copyright © 2012 by Miriam Mazzei

All rights reserved. No part of this book may be reproduced or transmitted in any form or by any means electronic or mechanical, including by photocopying, by recording, or by any information storage and retrieval system, without the express permission of the author and publisher, except where permitted by law.

Published in the United States of America
by Full Court Press, 601 Palisade Avenue
Englewood Cliffs, NJ 07632
www.fullcourtpressnj.com

ISBN 978-1-938812-02-6
Library of Congress Control No. 2012945922

Editing and Book Design by Barry Sheinkopf for Bookshapers
(www.bookshapers.com)

Colophon by Liz Sedlack

To *All* of our Wounded Warriors

who literally put life and limb on the line for us,
I dedicate this book.
Your sacrifice will *never* be taken for granted. "Thank you" isn't enough. May we find in ourselves a tiny portion of what it takes to make the ultimate sacrifices you have so bravely made. You honor us well and have made this country proud to be America.

To my personal mighty warrior, my son Brandon, to whom no words can express my love, pride,
and appreciation for what you have done and continue to do as you serve so proudly.

And to my own United States Navy disabled vet, my son Michael, who served this country well and kept your promise to come home alive.

Who are you now? Who is it you see?
I hear you say, "This is not me."
I see the stares. I hear the prayers,
People who say, "What was can't be."
But you were strong before it happened,
And you soon will be again.
For now, this is a setback.
But your living it did not end.

We know the road ahead is long.
It's hard, and it seems bleak.
But we will travel down it
Past all obstacles we meet.
But don't look back—you can't,
For then there is no balance.
To do so means to lose your way
And not to face the challenge.

    I am "just" a little child
    Of this you can be sure…

The pain, the shame, the guilt and all
The endless hard frustration—
"Don't let it show! Don't give a sign!"
You hide your desperation.
I see you as a powerful and strong
Determined warrior.
You aren't weak or helpless—
Discouraged, yes, yet still a hero.

Yes, you were there, you did your job,
Fulfilled your obligation,
And, now you're home, you won't complain-
For this is dedication.
It's the sounds, and those you left behind
That others cannot see.
You close your eyes and fall asleep.
Are you whole inside your dream?

    I am "just" a little child
    Of this you can be sure…

"I'll help you. Let me do that,"
You say. "I'll get the keys."
To hold a baby, catch a ball,
Each opportunity you seize.
The look in your eyes trying to hide
The pain of helplessness
Becomes your strength and courage
As you struggle for success.

You truly are a hero—
Of this there is no doubt.
But I will have to grow a bit
To figure all this out.
I watched you as you went away
Time and time again.
Now all this fear and loneliness
Have finally reached an end.

   I am "just" a little child
   Of this you can be sure…

As a hero, you must know
What a great thing you did.
Gratitude, pride, appreciation
Are hard to show a kid.
I watch you, see you make
Others feel better and smile.
Can I be like you
When I no longer am a child?

There are many others who
Come home different, too.
They also must start over,
Learning just like you.
Because they are true heroes,
Courageous, valiant, strong,
They will fight and not give up,
Be well before too long.

    I am "just" a little child
    Of this you can be sure…

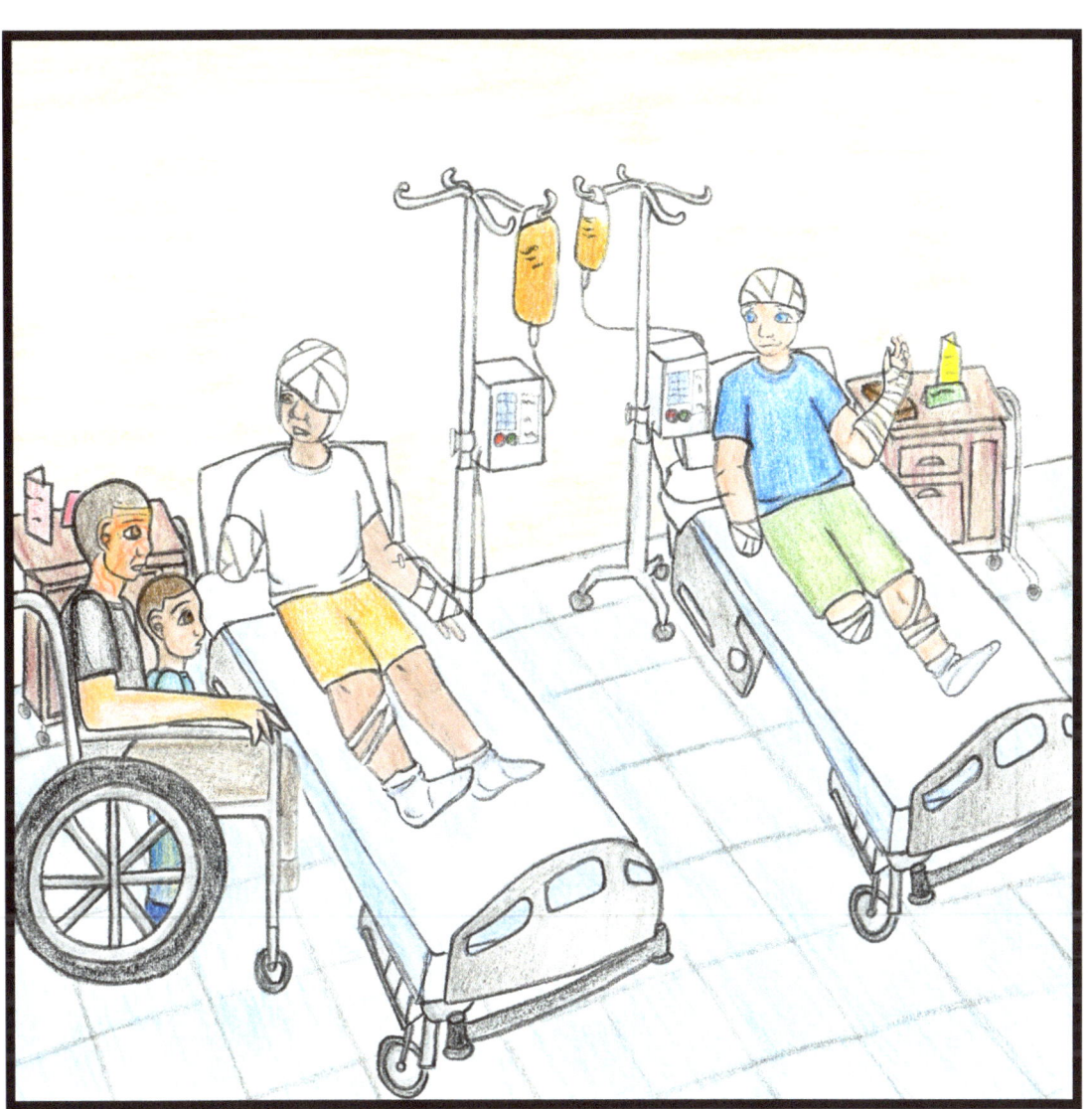

I hear that there's a name
For those who come home like you:
Strong, brave, loyal, sacrificing,
Faithful, determined, true.
These are the names that identify
Your special armor.
Now I know you are known
As a "Wounded Warrior".

I have learned the many ways
That you and others strived.
You fought to care for us,
Each other, and yet stay alive.
Sometimes it was hard to make
Choices that made you cry.
It's okay, Mommy. It's okay, Daddy.
We'll help your tears to dry.

You're the "Wounded Warrior," my hero.
   I am "just" a little child;
     Of this you can be sure…

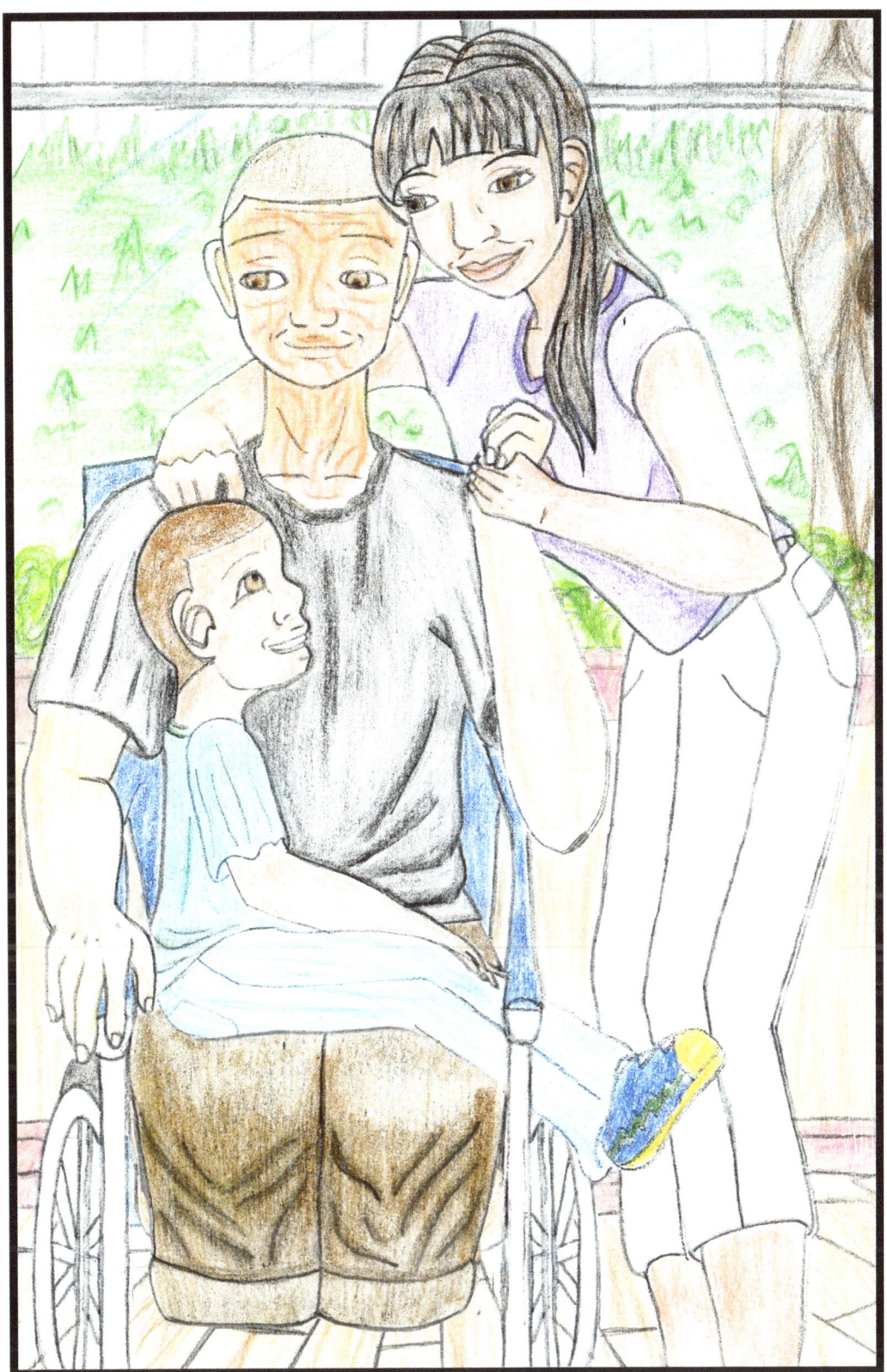

About the Author

Marie Parks Pinto, MSW, LSW, Psychiatric Psychotherapist, has over thirty years of experience involving children from birth to adulthood. A Certified Relationship Specialist and International Certified Christian Counselor, her expertise in parenting and childcare has led to appearances on the *Montel Williams Show*, participation in establishing the program Safe Haven, serving as a therapist for Dr. Phil, and being featured in the New Jersey Record. She is currently in private practice in association with a Neuro-forensic Psychiatrist in Bergen County.

Ms. Pinto has three adult sons and six grandchildren. Her second love of creative writing has been a lifelong dream, and she enjoys uniting her passion for it and for her professional work to provide knowledge and educational insights in an easy-to-read, nonclinical format that parents, children, and anyone involved with either can benefit from. That is her goal for this series.

About the Artist

At eighteen, Miriam Mazzei has had a few fun years of experience working with children, including those with special needs. She provided entertainment and homework help to grade schoolers while doodling on the side. Aside from high school art classes, she learned to draw on her own. This series gives her a perfect opportunity to combine her knowledge of children and love for drawing, and to share her passion with the rest of the world.